soft thorns
vol. II

also by bridgett devoue

soft thorns

soft thorns
vol. II

bridgett devoue

Andrews McMeel
PUBLISHING®

this book is dedicated to

the curious
the dreamers
and the strugglers

keep learning
keep dreaming
and keep fighting

because life offers more
for the fearless explorers
of the unknown

hello again

four years ago, my debut book, *Soft Thorns,* was released to the world. no one tells you to write a poetry book; the words have to burn so brightly in your soul that you're left with no other choice than to write them down or risk being burned alive. and it's from this fire that *Soft Thorns,* and my career as a poet, began.

i believe that part of being an artist is to live and retell your experiences through your work, so after *Soft Thorns* was published, i was hungry for life. i had just squeezed every last drop of my soul onto those pages, and i had a whole vessel to fill up again, the wax from which my flame would burn. so i set out on a journey to see where my passion would take me.

within these pages, you will come on that journey with me as we dive into moments of soul-aching longing, a romance that teeters on destruction, and the confusing world of saying goodbye. but this is much more than a love story; this is a book of questions. there will be some clear answers found within these pages, some answers will have to be found within yourself, and some answers may never truly be understood.

some of the things i write may have you yelling at the pages, passionately trying to shake me to do better. sometimes you will see your own story written in front of you. this is a good thing; it means you're in the right place. sometimes you'll have to question if what i wrote was really reality or simply my eyes bearing witness to what my heart yearned to see. all i can promise is that my words are as honest and vulnerable as i could be in that moment.

Soft Thorns isn't a collection of poems: it's crystallized moments, hung up forever on display like an art gallery of emotions. a secret place you have at your fingertips whenever you feel the urge to revisit and connect with another aching soul. *Soft Thorns* is always here for you, just as it has been for me.

one of the most important lessons i learned while filling up my vessel to write this book is that you (yes, you) are exactly what the world needs. your unique journey and set of experiences has lovingly caressed (and sometimes harshly battered) you into the inherently unique vessel that you are today. the world doesn't need another them; the world needs a you. we're all capable of spreading light in our own unique way to our own unique audience. my audience will be different than another poet's audience, and this is important, because if all the bees only stayed in the same field, flowers would never bloom anywhere else.

this reason is why i always try to inspire others to find their own light. *Soft Thorns* is not meant to be a self-indulgent dive into my life but an explorative journey together. me and you, exploring shared vulnerabilities that all humans hide deep within. i want to awaken the light within you as i learn to shine mine. *Soft Thorns* has always been a collaboration—my words and your heart—and i hope you enjoy going on this journey with me as much as i enjoyed writing it.

the world rewards those who let go and give in, so release yourself to my words, and let's begin.

xo bridgett

chapters

where you
left me

lying in the grass
gazing up at the sky
i wonder to myself

why i feel more at home
among the clouds
than i do among people?

maybe it's because
i know everything is temporary
and at least the clouds
don't try to hide it

she's soft like clouds
she'll let anyone
fall into her

the world feels heavy
for sensitive souls
because our hearts get
attached to things
that our minds know
will eventually end

hell is living a shallow existence
for a soul that craves depth

i'm forever battling
between being the person
others want me to be
and being the one
my heart needs me to be

i see broken people
all around me
and i can't help
but think

what a time to be in love

being the girl that
can have anyone
doesn't feel like it
alone in bed
at 4 a.m.

you're beautiful
means nothing
if looking in the mirror
you don't see beauty

i don't believe "angel"
is the right word to describe her
for angels don't dream
about playing with demons

and if she is an angel
then why is it so hard
for her to behave?

sometimes
i like to break
my halo in half
and wear it like horns
just to fit in
with my demons

and sometimes
i become more thorns
than roses
my petals hardening
into spears
making whoever
tries to hold me
bleed

sometimes i wonder
if i walk around
with a sign
around my neck
that reads

take advantage of me

i just want them
to feel special
like i never did
even if it means
that with them
i never will

maybe it's because they sense
that they already have me

maybe it's because i like bad boys
who treat me like my father did

i want the one
who has my heart
to make me feel
how i make them feel

special

but maybe that's the point
i'm simply not to them

and how many times
do i have to be
left on read
to understand this?

they say they love
my soft petals
but don't take the time
to learn how to make
my petals bloom

grabbing at me
through clenched fists
their selfish touch
damages me
making me harder to hold
for the next

did we forget that our words
can break people?

or do we simply not care?

or does our ego know
exactly what it's doing
destroying others' petals
so it doesn't have to share?

our deepest scars
are the ones hidden
so nobody knows
we have them

i get asked out
on a lot of dates
but they lose interest
when i tell them
it takes months for me
to feel comfortable
meeting physically

because my thorns
hold memories
of unwanted hands
tongue
teeth
and fingers
penetrating
my pleas
to stop

please

and i had
no one to blame but myself
they said

because this was not
an attack on the street

i had invited them in
and asked for
their company

my assault
was my own fault
in the eyes of others

so i vowed
to never let in
another attacker

because the only person
who can protect me
is me

when someone breaks your trust
their true nature is revealed
not by what they did
but by how they react

so when given no
explanation or apology
a thick fog of disappointment
hangs around their memory
in your head
distorting their voice
and the things they said

time is the only antidote
that will allow you to see clear
but in the moment
it's so disappointing
when you feel yourself
starting to breathe in
their toxic air

it's incredible
how hidden deep within me
lies the ability
to love someone else
yet loathe myself completely

i can't love many people
because they're not
broken enough for me
and i don't want
to be the one
to make them understand
what i mean

i crave words of devotion
from strangers
temporary validation
for the hurt i've felt
at the hands of others

maybe my father will love me now
and the scars from my rape won't last
and the sexual assaults will simply fade
into distant memories of my past

but i'm too scared to admit
for fear of lost attraction
that my past actions have made it
impossible to see love as anything
other than a transaction

i'm such a fool
and i'll die alone as such
nothing more than a memory
upon the lips of those
who never knew as much

i live in purgatory
where i want you
to want to
give me attention
but on my own time

maybe it's my insecurity
of not feeling worthy
or my obsessive need
to control everything

when you get too close
i crave space
but when you move too far
i long to keep you near

and i know
one day
i'll need to unlearn
all the habits that
got me here

i'm realizing now
i have an issue
with keeping relationships
healthy

for i tend to assimilate
into whatever that
persons needs
by mirroring their desires
and playing out their fantasies

but it happens
way too quickly for me
to feel reciprocation
that is genuine

and when i don't get
that energy back
i have nothing
left to give
not to you
and especially not to me

*because if it's not fulfilling
then it's draining*

there is no in-between

i give so much to others
that dating makes me feel
like i'm cheating on myself

you need to meet me physically
before you can know the real me

well i disagree

for i've met too many people
who do nothing but hiss lies
hypnotizing me with false charm
and serpentine eyes

yet my feline nature
makes me easy prey for snakes
because i'm far too curious
to not take their bait

so you show me your soul
and i'll show you mine
free from physical temptations
that blind us from seeing
if our hearts truly align

i simply need more intimacy
than taking off our clothes

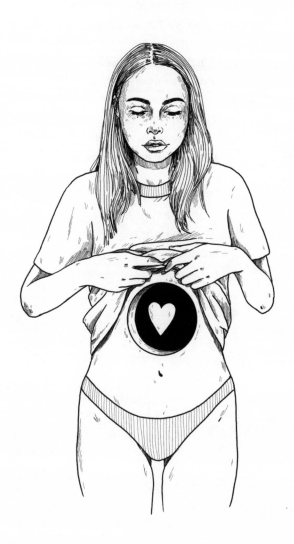

the amount of times
i've been deceived
by a person's true motives
and identity
makes me wonder

*when do you ever
really know a person?*

is it their fault
for lying just to get
what they want from me?

or is it my fault
for allowing myself
to only see
what i wanted to see?

communication is
everything to me
but without it
i'm left to assume
based on my past experiences
and that's where a beautiful thing
can turn ugly

is it too much to ask
for someone to simply
be excited that they
get to spend time
with me?

sometimes
we fall the hardest
for the things
we never had
because they never
had the chance
to disappoint us
like all the rest

even though
i let them hold me
they can never get too close
because i'm protected by
hidden thorns

love me for me
or don't love me at all

and here i am
once again
alone at 2 a.m.
drowning in love to give
knowing that the people
i want to swim with
refuse to get in

it's not a coincidence
that i keep finding myself
in this predicament

but falling in love
with someone unavailable
feels like a safe bet
because they won't
break my heart
since they refuse to
ever hold it
to begin with

i want to rush to the part
where we become one and
take on the world together
to experience what
i've seen in the movies
implanted into my brain
as the key to happiness
from a young age
by Disney

it starts by changing
little things

a different hour of sleep
a different style of dress
a different list of things i like
obsessing over the size of my chest

and slowly
i'll lose my own
identity
until the person staring back
has become
an enemy

maybe this is why
my relationships don't last
when inevitably
i realize i'm drowning
and i'm the only one
who can save myself

and if i perceive
even a hint of disinterest
i'm shattered because
i've overinvested
into something when
i should have been
more cautious

*relationships don't have to be toxic
to be bad for our health*

i often wonder
if i'm too romantic
for this world

while everyone around me
prizes marriage and stability
i crave passion so fiery
it burns the world down
until it's just us two

i want to get so lost together
that we give up trying to
come back to reality
and just make our own instead

i want a reckless romance
not afraid to test the limits
of what human connection
can reach

and even if
i have to risk everything
it's worth it to feel love
from the highest peak

i always fall in love
with those moments
that live in between
words and actions

where silence
sets the stage
for our souls to be
the main attractions

our hearts are reckless
and whose fault is that?

theirs for foolishly falling
or ours for saying
we'll catch them?

when i look inside me
all that i can see
are broken parts
rusty from abuse
dusty from lack of use
and i get worried that i'll
never love again

but sometimes
someone i meet
shows my broken heart
that it still knows
how to beat

i'm reminded that
i was born to do this

looking into the abyss
of steel and lights
i know you're there
because i can feel you
thinking of me

and if you're not in that abyss
then i'll look to the one
in the stars
and find solace
in the fact
that no matter
what happens here
we will inevitably be together
forever
one day

maybe i've thought
about meeting you so much
that you've started to feel
like a familiar memory

am i any different
from that little girl
who dreamed of you?

she still lives within me
seeing what i see
dreaming what i dream
or maybe she's the one
who's still dreaming for me

the one who holds
control of my heart
twisting it
giving me that little spark
the one who
makes me wonder

is this finally you?

*love in
the chaos*

it's amazing
how love can change
the way we view the world
and most importantly
ourselves

i hope you know
that i'm broken too
but i'm going to keep
fighting for you

because there has to be
more to this life
than we thought we knew

*i felt it when i looked
into your eyes*

i fell in love with you
because your broken
matched my broken

only you
can make my
heart flutter
while falling
and keep me grounded
while flying

i try to write poetry about you
but i can never find the words
because you open within me
emotions that have yet
to be defined
by humanity

and i just wonder
one day
if you'll think of me
the same way

i want to crawl into that
dark place of yours
and shine your light
by reflecting in me
your beauty i see
so you finally feel
how worthy of love
you are to me

i'll risk breaking
my glued-together heart
if it means
you'll put it back together
with your loving touch
the way it was
always meant to be
from the very start

i want to die in your arms
leave behind the problems
of this world
and be reborn
into a new one
of our own creation

you're an angel
because you're not afraid
of my demons

people who say
oceans are endless
have never felt
your love

from the moment
i met you
i knew i wanted
your hands around
my neck

such devilish thoughts
for an angel to have

a curious angel
just wanted to know
what it felt like
to play with a demon

so she traded in
her halo and wings
for lingerie and other
sinful things

out of sight
hidden under white
she wore his mark
like a tattoo
her demon's bite

i feel like an angel
around you
because all the
sinning we do
feels so good

*you make me
want to behave*

we wouldn't have
this much chemistry
if we weren't
supposed to use it

i just blushed
so fucking hard
i think i got
a little high

is it possible to
overdose on desire?

let me trace your thorns
with my fingers

and

my

petals

fell

you've taken hold of my heart
you're my 3 a.m. thought
unlocking another side of me
that only you get to see
and who knows

i might even be more
sinful than you

the way you make me feel
i don't think i'm supposed
to like it

but i'm addicted to your touch
fingertips dragging down my soul
you're burning me whole
reminding me that i'm even
alive at all

lust is addictive
fingertips dancing
on flames

like every breath
has meaning

*inhale pleasure
exhale pain*

i don't need therapy
i just need you
with your cocaine lips
and your lidocaine kiss

when i'm with you
i feel numb to my pain

no matter how many times
i've been down this road
walked by the same signs
warning me to turn back

i still walk it

because hope holds
her hands over my eyes
while blissful ignorance
takes hold of mine

a gentle guide back
to my destruction

i don't just fall in love
instead i climb
to the highest peak

and breathe deep

diving in
even deeper
yet forgetting to ask
if you also wanted
to take this leap

he exists somewhere
between comfort and fear
in my heart

just a pendulum swing
from running away
or falling in love

you say you have
a sharp tongue
but you forget

i like pain

you're the type of guy
i'll take however i can get
even if that means with you
breaking my heart

you told me
i was like fine china

beautiful to look at
yet more beautiful
for how easily
i can break

you loved the risk
of holding me
knowing you held
full control over
my fate

i think i like you more now
knowing you have the power
to break my heart

lust blinds you
while love let's you see
and if this is only lust
then i will stay blind
to the obvious signs
of how wrong you are
for me

you don't scare me
because i want you
to ruin me

i've been numb
for so long that
i just want to feel
something

*you light my
soul on fire
and i only hope
you can handle
my flame.*

the art of destruction

you said
i just want to be casual
and became a murderer

your words
the weapon
and our romance
the casualty

you don't want me
to try so hard with you
but you don't understand
that once i stop trying
you'll never hear from me again

*because me focusing on me
means letting you go*

we want love
but we don't want to
work together
to be in love

*we expect our flower to bloom
yet refuse to water it*

i love your beautiful mind
you're one of a kind
and the one for me
but you'll never see

because i pretend
i don't count the minutes
until you text
and i pretend to laugh along
when you tell me about your ex
and i pretend to be ok
that we don't cuddle after sex

because i'm that cool girl
just one of the dudes girl
no strings attached
not complex

so i learned to love you
like injecting lidocaine
shutting off my brain
forgetting what you say
so i'm numb the next time
when you run away

you don't have to
share me with anyone else
and that's why i feel like
i shouldn't have to share you

you get all of me
and all i ask
is for the same in return

am i selfish?

remember the days
when we first spoke?

how naturally
our magic flowed?

but if you say
that this is love
then what was that?

i would trade in
love any day
just to get
our spark back

together
we were burning ourselves alive
but apart
it's like i'm barely living

just two different ways to die

it's tragic
how two people
can be perfect for each other

but not in this lifetime

i'm grateful for my delusions
for even though
i can only be in love
with the thought of you
because you won't let me
love all of you

i'm still happy as if
you were mine

my angel eyes
see a fantasy
and believe it could be
the real thing

so i fell for you
without knowing your truth
until one day
i closed my eyes
and saw the devil in you

i'm breaking with you
but i'm scared to find out
how much more i'll break
without you

if you're not going
to let down your walls
and give me your full heart
then please don't waste my time

because i'm addicted to love
with a high tolerance
so i need a full dose
to still get me high

so let's just stay friends
because i'd rather be sober
than get half your love
and keep wondering why

why seduce me
with sweet nothings
when your intentions
were always bitter?

around you
i'm acutely aware
of how damaged i am
because your light
shines on my scars
making them impossible
to blend in

am i proud of my rejections
carved into my skin?

or my verbal lashings from my father
making me feel i don't deserve to live?

why hide them when
we all have scars covering our skin?

because no one else shows them
and we all just want to fit in

so i would show you
but i don't want more scars
because even though
staying numb isn't living
i don't know if i have
any room left
on my body
for you

you keep asking me to fall
promising you'll catch me
without knowing the weight
of the burdens i carry

for you have no idea
how truly heavy i feel

my heart knows
this won't work out
so even though
i'm still with you

i'm already missing you

this isn't a relationship

this is both of us
trying to walk away
looking like
the better person

i realize now
we were never really in love

because you broke my heart
before i even got a chance
to touch yours

sometimes angels
are just demons
wearing halos

instead of trying to build
a relationship with me
you just complained
about our lack of one

i write these poems
to have the conversations
i'm too scared to have
with you

*connection was all i ever
craved from you*

*and the one thing
you could never fake*

you told me
we're going to burn together

so you lit a match
and set me ablaze
watching me burn with that
smirk on your face

but then you turned around
and just walked away

some people like
to watch the world burn
but to you

the world was already burning

it's so painful
when you just want
to love someone
but they don't even know
what love is

each loving touch
is a scratch on the walls
they've built up
an attack on their defense

and fight back you did

i've discovered
a new most terrible
feeling

falling in love
yet not being able
to fully experience it

i don't remember
the last time
i felt truly happy
since you arrived
in my life

you stole all
the happiness from me
so you weren't alone
in your misery

we never know
how fragile someone
is until they break

the amount of times
i've been on the phone with you
tears silently streaming
down my face

and you never noticed
because you don't listen
to me with your heart
since you only ever
learned to love me
with your eyes

and as these tears fall
i'm falling out of love with you

the scariest emotion
i've ever faced
was your jealousy

a war waged against
your own ego
while you assaulted me
saying i was the enemy

this hurts too much
to even write down
because i know what
my pen writes is true
and i don't want to admit
what my reality has become
with you

i fall asleep every night
with tears in my eyes
the happy thoughts of us
escaping down my cheeks
running from the toxicity
of what we've become
in my memory

i'm crying
not because i'm losing
what we have now
but because i'm losing
what we could have been

i don't know
if i'm strong enough
to keep being
in love with you

why do you make it
so impossibly hard
to just love you?

it wasn't the abuse

it was the fact
the abuse
was from you

how can something so beautiful
cause so much pain?

because your love was like
a razor blade
your sharp tongue
excited me
a challenge to take
your lashings
and show you
how strong i could be

prove to you that i'm worthy

but i didn't equate
that maybe you simply
liked giving out pain
and i had become
your perfect prey

i remember when
your lidocaine kiss
used to numb me
from my pain

*and now
you just numb me
from my happiness*

if i say goodbye to you
then i'm saying goodbye
to everything we've built
and i don't know
what's scarier to me

to lose you
or lose our memories

i don't remember
my life without you
so how can i go on in life
without you?

i worry if i give in to
what my heart wants
i'll lose whatever grasp
on reality i have left

but then i look at what
my reality has become

so i take a deep breath
and jump

now that i'm living
my worst fear
i'm no longer scared
because when you're faced
with no other choice
than to jump off that cliff

*the fall becomes
your friend*

staring up at me
suddenly
unassumingly

my fears solidified
as tiny letters on a screen

so here it is

and no matter
how much my fingers
tap my screen
in search
of the hope
suffocating under
a mountain of
unsaid feelings

this is goodbye.

the final
goodbye

you were my first
and you probably
won't be my last

but every time
my lips meet lips
and the hands
on my hips
slowly tighten
their grasp

all i can feel is you
and what we used to do

and now my body's gone cold
remembering you and me
are through

the feeling of rejection
is one that's hard
to reconcile with

because even your own soul
is too embarrassed to admit it

as the voices in your head smirk
i told you so

i don't believe in
falling in love quickly
with a person
but i do believe
in falling in love quickly
with a fantasy

read souls
not words

even though
i want you
to want me
and to fight for you
to love me

it's easier on my heart
to let go knowing why
than to allow you
to go in silence

have you ever
broken your own heart
trying to avoid
a broken heart?

sorry i wasn't ready
but i knew to love you
would be like opening
pandora's box

one kiss
would ruin every other
kiss for me

yet ironically
i'm still ruined
carrying the burden
of knowing
i let go of the one

i hated who
i was becoming
so i had to leave you
even if i hated
doing it

sometimes when
you're talking to someone
you're not actually
talking to them

you're speaking to their ego
while they're speaking to yours

and i'm not sure if
we ever really spoke

people will try
to justify their jealousy
and actions toward you
by rewriting history
in their minds
but words leave scars
that can never be erased
from the heart

you held my heart
how you thought you should
not how you truly wanted to

if you ever even wanted to

we had become actors
mimicking the motions
of scenes we had seen

our relationship
nothing more than
an empty stage

a rehearsal for the real thing

i thought you would
be in my life forever
and you are

as my biggest mistake

you were my venom
and i'm my only antidote

i had already
let go of you
we stopped speaking
six months ago

but now i need to let go
of the hope that one day
you might look at me
like i could be yours

so i'm letting you know
that i'm letting you go
to make space
for someone who does

looking down at my collection
of newly formed scars
i think to myself

you might be gone
but you certainly
left your mark

i have a ritual
every time my phone rings
my heart skips a beat
and i savor the excitement
of the possibility
that it could be you saying

come home to me

so i wait twenty minutes
and then twenty more
to live in this reality
that you actually loved me

foolish in love
and even more foolish in loss

i think about you
less and less each day
and that makes me sad

because even though
it wasn't real
and even though
you never asked
my love for you
got me through
some of the most difficult
moments of my past

i put down the knife
because of you

smiled at myself in the mirror
because of you

let my heart out of its cage to fly free
because of you

maybe one day i'll tell you

one day
when the cuts don't sting

one day
when we've both found others
to fill the empty spots in our beds
and the emptier holes left
from abandoning our
shared dreams

maybe then
we can talk and pretend
that we weren't both scared
to fall in love
because we knew
it would be

the end

you showed me true love
and i ran

because it's an emotion
i had never felt before
and how could i be
anything other than
an impostor
for accepting a gift
i didn't feel
worthy of yet

maybe you exposed me
to this kind of love
so i'll be ready
for the next one

but deep down
i hope you'll stick around
so the next one is you

i was so scared
of letting you down
i didn't realize
this whole time
i had been
letting myself down

sometimes we stay
in toxic relationships
to stay distracted
from the painful reality
that it's us
who need to improve

i'm sorry it seemed
like i didn't trust you

it's just that i was always
looking for rejection
in all of your actions

because i didn't believe
i was capable of being loved

it's not your fault
i couldn't love you

i never learned what love was
because i didn't care enough
to fall in love with myself

i don't think
anyone's even fallen
for the real me
just a fantasy
but who am i to blame
when that's all
i'll ever let them see

don't be afraid
to use your thorns
when you need to

*your petals won't be
any less soft*

your presence
made me strong
but your absence
makes me stronger

the best feeling ever
is when you're finally
over someone
you shouldn't have been into
in the first place

i used to be sad that i lost you
but now i'm sad for you
that you lost me

people may come and go
but your heart doesn't know this

like a young child
throwing a tantrum
ignorant to the pain she'll feel
and the damage she's caused
when she realizes
she has no other choice
than to give in

hearts don't age with years
they age through scars

demons are misunderstood
for they get lonely too
like all of us do

and maybe they're just
looking for friends
to be accepted
in the right hands

for all their ugly flaws
might just be beautiful
with the right perspective

when someone
shows you their demons
they're giving you
the opportunity
to heal them

we're all damaged
even if we can't see
the unique formation of cracks
forming under the surface
breaking apart our souls
but connecting us together
in the shared trauma
of life

i believe love is
transferable energy

so keep that emotion
that's found a home
in your heart
and transfer it
to someone more
deserving

letting go is part of loving too
so practice loving yourself
by letting go of
what's hurting you.

*(re)finding
the light*

i sometimes find myself
unable to accept
the good in my life
because i'm too focused
on bracing myself
for when it's
eventually gone

a child of trauma
just waiting for the next blowup

but everything in life
is temporary
and the only way
you can control it
is to change the way
you view it

we hold onto
our moments of rejection
like a report card of
a list of our failures

so when we meet someone new
we can show them

this is why i can't be loved

but i'm exhausted
with having to carry
the weight of the grades
others gave me

rejection in whose eyes?

because i believe
i'm still standing

although revisiting moments
of rejection may sting
it's important to see things
logically
by taking our emotions out
to appreciate our growth
instead of focusing
on the details of
the journey

what we say always matters
because regardless of the size
a cut is still a cut
and we never know
how many scars are hidden
under someone's skin

we hold the power
to plant seeds of hope
in the gardens of others
or destroy their roses
with toxic waters

low points are
the most powerful
moments in our lives
for these are the best times
to make a change

when we have
nothing left to lose
that's when we gain
the fearless attitude
needed to transform
our hearts in gratitude

it's ok to ask for help
for sometimes
we all need
a little saving
from ourselves

when we start honoring
our true selves
we start shedding people
like a snake

don't be alarmed
trust the process

everyone is lonely
which is why miserable people
try to make you
miserable with them

but if you surround yourself
with people you admire
then they will elevate you
to their level
to feel less alone

sometimes it's easier
to miss someone
than have them
in our lives
waiting patiently until
the time is right

because i spent my life
searching for forever
only to realize
that destiny would
lead me there
inevitably
so everything else is
perfectly temporary

and at least
i still have my thoughts
of you to keep
me company

am i the only one
who can fall this deeply
in love with a memory?

you can't make
someone love you
you can only make them
want to love you

*so love with magnets
instead of glue*

imagine if we could see
a time line of how long
a relationship will last

a note of death perhaps?
would this make us feel
less bad?

for sometimes
we will walk through life
with a companion
and sometimes
they go their own path

but flowers blooming
are always beautiful
even if they're not
in the same garden

we must remember
that we don't see ourselves
the way others do

for our perspective
stays blinded by
an internal sense of dread
and the demons in our head

*we are the book
and the world is reading us*

there's beauty living
within our pages
that we can't see
so we must trust others
to read it for us

your heart is a library
filled with novels
about the people
you love

and even if they're
no longer in your life
the love you once felt
can be found within
these pages

available for you
to reread on
a rainy afternoon
when you need
their warm embrace

part of loving someone
is letting them go
while letting them know
they forever have a space
in your heart's library
bookmarked for
their return

i think we feel lonely
because we all started out
indistinguishable from the next

threads woven into the
fabric of the universe
breathing one breath

until the day
we broke apart from the rest
to enter these human bodies
and put our spirits to the test

only to spend our lives
craving to be interwoven
like the threads
we started as

this time on earth
is for exploring
your individualism
because we already
have a home
for indistinguishable
connectedness

nature is full of contradictions
so why in humans
is this considered bad?

our contradictions give us
the strength to adapt
but society likes to
put us in boxes
because they're the ones
who control the lids

i reject
society's attempt
to put me in a box
and label me as
something i am not

for roses can only
grow so much
when their petals keep
getting crushed

it's not selfish to be
selfish with our time
because time is life's currency
and if we spend it on
empty calories
that don't satisfy us spiritually
then we'll just be living life
emotionally hungry

*we must feed ourselves first
in order to have the energy
to feed others*

sometimes healing
hurts more than
the injury itself
because initial pain is fast
but healing refuses to rush

and this is a good thing

for we earned these scars
on our bodies and our hearts

if all humans are flawed
then our flaws aren't flaws

we're simply human

what we consume
is what we become

and i wonder
how we would be
if we could physically see
the effect that it has on
our hearts
our souls
and our bodies?

if we could see it rotting us away
a self-induced cancer
eroding our spirit
like metal to water

would we continue
to use poison
to water our roses
or seek out something
more nourishing
to make our petals bloom?

my deepest scars
weren't made by big wounds
but small cuts

my father telling me
i'll never make him proud
his disappointed face
burned into my memory

the anxiety of looking out
at a cafeteria full of my peers
and not having any friends
to sit with

the hollowness of going home
from a stranger's house at 9 a.m.,
knowing he won't ever
text me again

bridgett devoue

in a garden
we tend to focus on
the big pests
and sometimes forget
about the smaller weeds
that over time
destroy our roses

these subtle moments
are vines that wrap
around our hearts
and enslave our confidence

*by clearing our gardens
we can finally see
the full beauty of what
we can blossom into being*

there are not enough words
in the English language
to explain our feelings

for there exists an infinite
number of emotions
between grief and love
happiness and sadness
longing and mourning
that we have yet to name

but that doesn't make
the emotions we feel
any less real

the finite nature of language
does not limit the vastness
of your expression

so even if you feel
like a confusing mess
a mash-up of definitions
fighting for dominance
and you can't even
find the words
to describe it to your friends
find solace in knowing
that there exist some
emotions so powerful
that words would only serve
to devalue them

you seem to have everything
so it's ok to bring you down

even though you've traveled
to your darkest corners
and know intimately
the baggage you carry

some will still choose
to only see you
as nothing more than what
they can personally view

they will try to
justify their actions
of attacking you
by saying you hold
something of value

but they're nothing more
than petty thieves
and there's a compliment hidden
through their cleaned teeth

i'm jealous because
you are what i cannot be

there's comfort in knowing
that beauty can be found
in everything

because in good moments
things are good
and in bad moments
things will grow

so when our eyes
begin to adjust
to this new perspective's light
it's like being able to see
for the very first time

we all share the same fate
and how foolish we are
that even with this knowledge
we still find ways to hate

every second
is nothing short
of a miracle
and the tragedy of life
is that we're taught
to forget this

if you're going to be
unapologetically yourself
then inevitably
you're going to feel
that gnawing scratch

but this is a different kind
of loneliness

solitude is the humble purity
of the human experience

they will constantly try
to dull your shine
because they are intimated
by your light

but remember
you were meant to shine
like the stars you're made of

we must always stay
young in our hearts
for youth is defined by
an insatiable curiosity

once the necessity for learning ends
so does purpose

and the human body
is simply a shell
for the fire that burns
deep within

it doesn't make sense
to fight against the currents
when the river will always
take us to the same place
so enjoy the journey
flowing with the waves

i need time
he needs time
the rose needs time
love needs time

money buys time
but the media will try

you're running out of time
to poison our minds

and marketing schemes
have no influence
over your worthiness
of getting this gift
bestowed upon every creation
that ever exists

time is the currency
of the universe
and life is cashing in

and death is
the enemy of time
so all the more
reasons why
there is no reason
to rush to die

for eventually the funds
will run out
and you will take
your last breath
so enjoy life like it's
a vacation from death

if you were locked in a prison
and only you held the key
would you let yourself out
or stay behind bars
indefinitely?

fear is a response
from your body
to keep you safely
in your comfort zone
away from harm

but also from greatness

we hold ourselves back
with excuses
until one day
our will to live
will become greater
than our fears

every rose has its story
every thorn has a purpose

but sometimes
they can no longer hurt us
and that's when they become

soft thorns

acknowledgments

to those who believed in me
thank you for never giving up on my vision. your
love and support motivated me to put my heart
out into the world again and publish this book.

to those who didn't believe in me
my pain is the water from which i blossom,
so thank you for helping me become the rose
i am today.

social media

Join Bridgett Devoue on the following:

- @bridgettdevoue
- @bridgettdevoue
- @bridgettdevoue
- @bridgettdevoue
- @bridgett
- @bridgettdevoue

Find more of Laura Klinke's work here:

- @lauraklinke_art

Enjoy *soft thorns vol. II* as an audiobook narrated by the author, wherever audiobooks are sold.

Andrews McMeel Publishing
a division of Andrews McMeel Universal
1130 Walnut Street, Kansas City, Missouri 64106

www.andrewsmcmeel.com

Illustrations by Laura Klinke, @lauraklinke_art

21 22 23 24 25 BVG 10 9 8 7 6 5 4 3 2 1

ISBN: 978-1-5248-6695-2

Library of Congress Control Number: 2018942776

Editor: Patty Rice
Art Director: Spencer Williams
Production Editor: Elizabeth A. Garcia
Production Manager: Cliff Koehler